I0759862

PALMISTRY

ANCIENT WISDOM
FOR THE NEW AGE

PALMISTRY

THE SECRET OF THE HAND

Olga Lempiinska

Text, illustrations, and photographs by IMM Lifestyle Books, an imprint of Fox Chapel Publishing, 903 Square Street, Mount Joy, PA 17552. *www.foxchapelpublishing.com*

First published in 1998 by New Holland (Publishers) Ltd

Designed and edited by
Complete Editions
40 Castelnau
London SW13 9RU

Editorial Direction: Yvonne McFarlane
Editor: Michèle Brown
Designer: Peter Ward

ISBN 978-1-5048-0160-7

Printed in China
First Printing

CONTENTS

ACROSS THE MILLENIA

Whether graced by the grand titles of chirognomony, the study of the overall shape of the hand, or chiromancy, the study of the lines, people have been fascinated by the hand for thousands of years, both as the means by which much of everyday life is made feasible and as a reflection of the inner self.

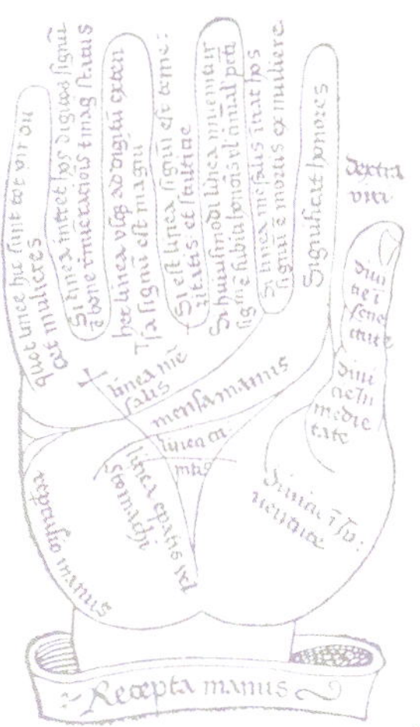

Though there is little recorded history until the time of Aristotle, it is thought that the ancient Chinese studied the hand as early as the third century bc. In India, soon after this time, hand analysis was recorded in scientific records such as the monumental *Shastra*. Written by Aryan sages, and also known as

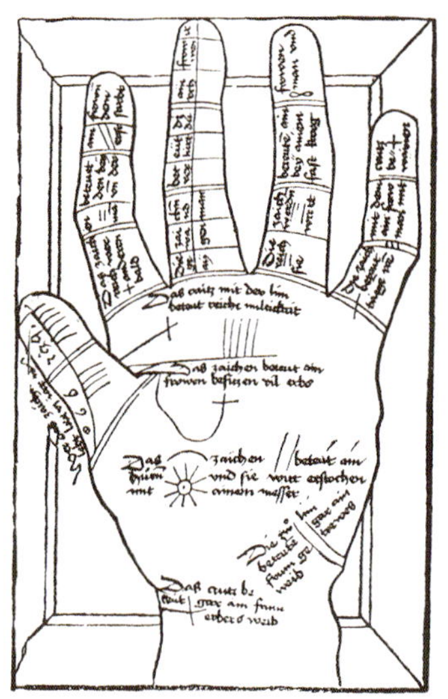

the Vedic texts, it also included readings of the head, chest and feet. Our early knowledge of Ayurvedic medicine comes from these texts. The popularity of palmistry in the near and middle east also suggests a long history which has been passed down through the Chaldeans, Sumerians and Babylonians.

The ancient Greeks were keen students of the hand, and several sources record that Aristotle found an ancient Arabic treatise on the hand on an altar to Hermes, which he sent to his most distinguished pupil, Alexander the Great.

Anaxagoras, the Greek thinker, propounded that man's superiority over other animals was due to the ability to use his hands. In his *Treatise on the Parts of Animals*, Aristotle devotes a section to a criticism of this belief in which he rates man's overall superior intelligence, which gave him the intellect to use his hands, as a more important fact in man's superiority. He concludes that the hand is talon, hoof and horn at will. It is the sword and spear or whatever weapon you please. He also discoursed on the importance of nails. Man has them for protection, whilst base animals use them solely for fighting. Aristotle's thoughts look dubious today, but the fact that the hand was given so much attention shows how important it is in the scheme of things.

The Romans were interested in hands, along with almost every other possible type of divination. Artemidorus wrote a treatise, now lost, which must have been of considerable importance if it matched the content of his *Interpretation of Dreams*. Josephus, the Jewish historian, recorded that Julius Caesar was skilled at reading hands and that "it was impossible for any man whose palm Caesar had seen to deceive him in any way. One day a man came to him claiming to be the son of King Herod. Caesar recognised him as an imposter immediately as he had no sign of royalty on his hand."

The hand appears significantly in the Bible with specific references to palmistry in Proverbs 3:16 'Length of days is in her right hand; and in her left hand riches and honour'. In Exodus there is a reference to the hand as symbolising God's presence and power and it is still the custom for the blessing to be given with the thumb, index and middle fingers raised, evoking the Father, Son and Holy Ghost.

The practice of the laying on of hands crosses all faiths and continents, from Native Americans to priests in Nepal.

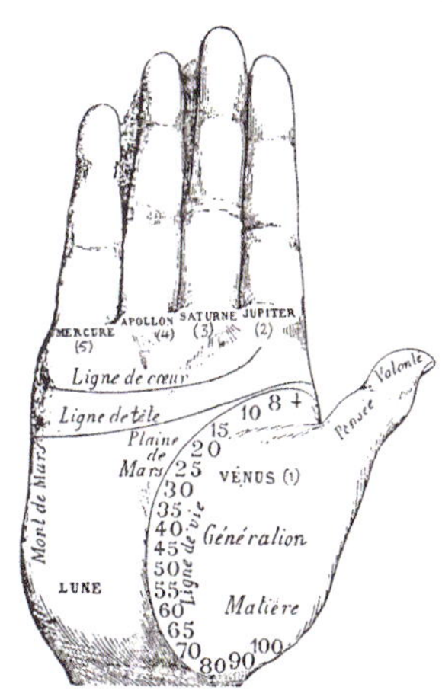

However, it was not until the 19th century that palmistry began to be recorded in a systematic way. The most influential writers were the French chiromancers, D'Arpentigny and Desbarolles, who laid down the basic rules for classifying hands. D'Arpentigny classified the major types of the hand in 1843, a system still followed today.

From China 5000 years ago to the computer age, the hand, with its hills and valleys, roads and streams, provides a map of life's terrain to guide us to a greater understanding of our inner feelings and potential achievements.

HAND AND MIND

There are five specific types of hand which should be studied in general before embarking on a reading of the various features, including the nails, the phalanges, the joints, the lines and the mounts. There are two general types of hand, the first being delicate when first examined and related to the conic type. It is a receptive hand, welcoming ideas and emotional currents. The second is of firmer appearance, representing a more outgoing and assertive type, realistic in all matters.

The flexibility of the hand must first be noted and general consistency, which can range from flabby, which suggests low energy levels, to hard, which reacts against the reader's pressure. This suggests a lack of mental agility and a generally inflexible nature. In between, there are flexible hands, which reflect vitality and openness of mind.

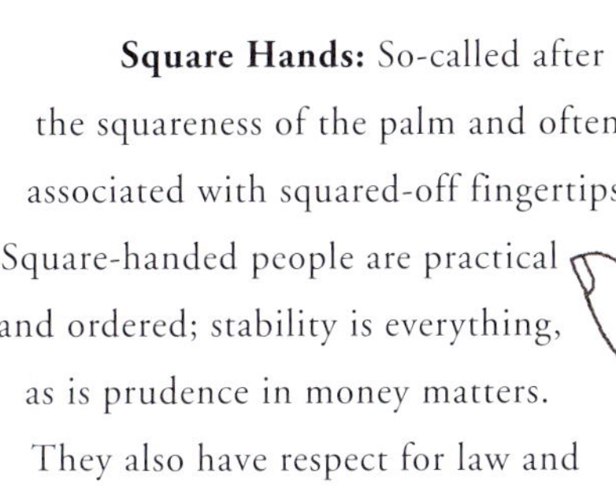

Square Hands: So-called after the squareness of the palm and often associated with squared-off fingertips. Square-handed people are practical and ordered; stability is everything, as is prudence in money matters. They also have respect for law and order. The only order they don't like is that imposed by office work.

Spatulate Hands: Narrower at the wrist but squaring towards the fingers, these hands are also realistic, but with a more positive approach to action. Spatulate-handed people are practical, but impulsive; tenacious, but innovative. They show extroversion and self-confidence. They are always on the go, inventing, building, wheeler-dealering. But beware. When the hand is also flexible, they can be diverted by sensual pleasures.

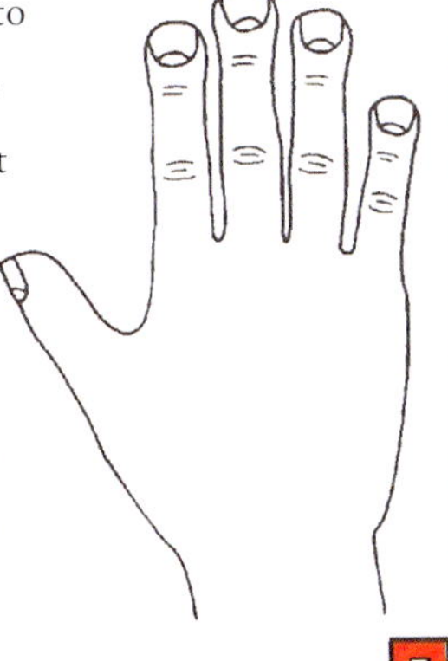

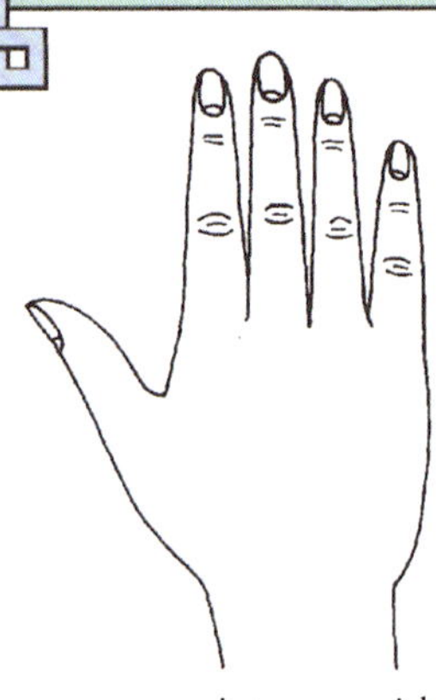

Conical Hands: The shape is moving to a more rounded appearance, more feminine and overtly artistic. Creative flair is in abundance and the nature of people with such hands is capricious, impulsive and romantic. They can pick new ideas out of the air and take up new interests with great ease. When the hand is firm, the mind is active, when the hand is fat, the libido takes control.

Psychic Hands: The least common hand is possessed by dreamers and visionaries. The long look, with elegantly pointed tips, is the extension of the conic ideal. Feelings prevail and sensitivity is paramount, leading to introversion. They are impractical and unrealistic and need help to cope with the material world. If the fingers have exaggerated knuckles, they are ethical and moral thinkers.

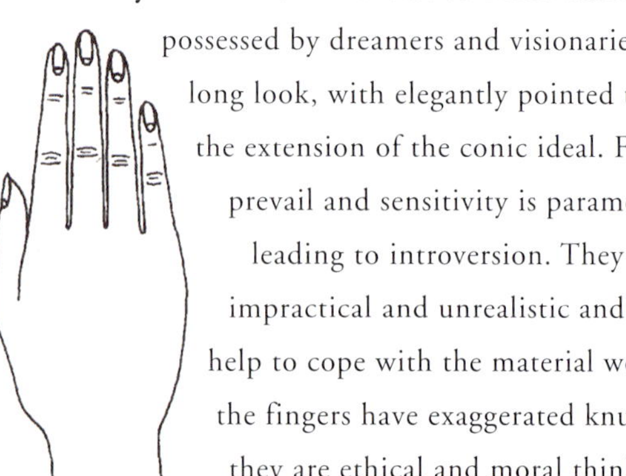

The Mixed Hand: This is the hand most people have. This example is one of the infinite variations possible when the many elements – basic palm shape, types of fingers, length of phalanges, angle of the thumb and the prominence of the mounts – are taken into account.

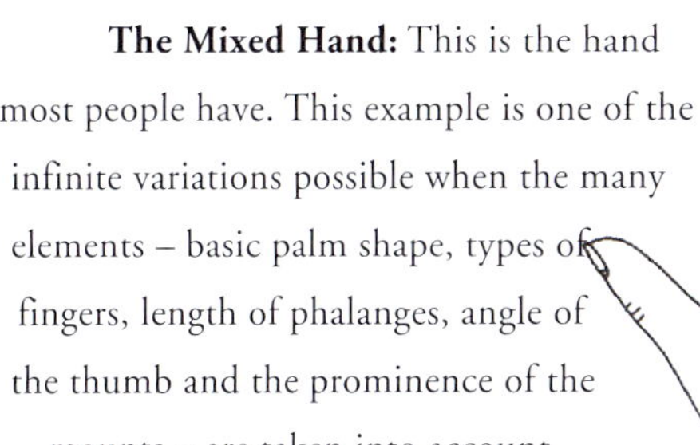

WHICH HAND?

It is popularly thought that the left hand is what you're born with and the right hand is what you make of yourself. To accept this is to completely miss the point of how the brain functions. The left hemisphere of the brain deals with practicalities, logic, writing, speech and so on. The right hemisphere is the creative part. As brain messages cross over the body, the right hemisphere governs the left-hand side of the body and vice versa. From this we can conclude that the active, right hand tells us about the conscious self, whilst the left reveals the unconscious, even the unrealised. For a left-handed person this is reversed.

MOUNTS AND MEANINGS

The mounts of the hand are named after the planets and reflect the mythological qualities associated with them.

The Mount of Venus (1), named after the Goddess of Love, is the area at the base of the thumb, under which the main blood vessel of the hand runs. This relates it to passion and health.

The Mount of Jupiter (2), named after the king of the gods, also known as Zeus, is at the base of the first finger. It represents ambition, enthusiasm and a will to win.

The Mount of Saturn (3) lies at the base of the second finger and relates to the need for solitude and indicates a studious frame of mind.

The Mount of the Sun (4) is at the base of the third finger and is also called the Mount of Apollo. It indicates artistic sensibilities and imaginative qualities.

The Mount of Mercury (5), at the base of the little

finger, is named after the messenger of the gods and indicates personal and professional communication skills.

There are two **Mounts of Mars** (**6** and 7). Both reflect the qualities of the god of war. The Upper Mount, found below the Mount of Mercury, shows personal determination. The Lower Mount, between the Mounts of Jupiter and Venus, shows self-assertion. The Mount of Luna (8), opposite the Mount of Venus, above the wrist, relates to subconscious drives and unconscious instincts.

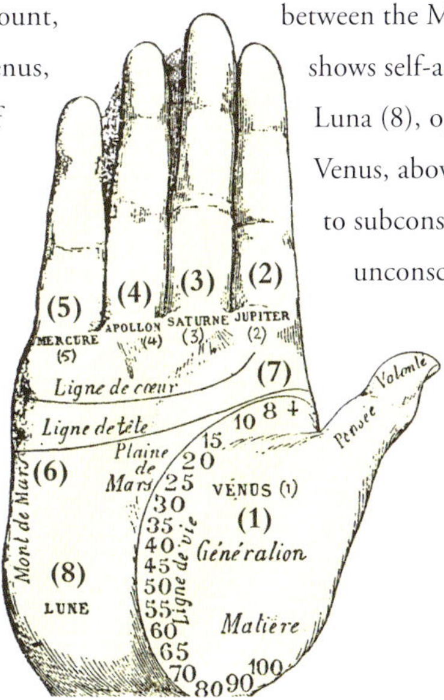

As with all the features of the hand, the mounts are affected by the lines and features which define and cross them.

The Mount of Venus. The most influential of the mounts is often thought to influence all the others. With the life line defining it at the ball of the thumb, it should have no extreme features, such as being too bold, too lined or too big, which would presage over-indulgence on several fronts. It should be higher than all the others, emphasising a joy for life and love. Well shaped within the life line is an omen for a good long life, even

if the line itself appears flawed. An underdeveloped Venus, flat and small, shows lack of vitality and passion and a cold, introverted nature.

The Mount of Jupiter. A gregarious and outgoing personality is reflected, together with charisma and inspirational qualities. Leadership ability, akin to Leo in astrology, in politics, business or social life, can border on the obsesssive if the mount is too prominent. Complemented by sympathetic fingers and lines, a true leader is at hand, whilst a flat mount shows limited self-esteem, ambition and social skills.

The Mount of Saturn. This shows the inner search for truth, with a healthy gift of self-appraisal. Saturn is the judge, between independence and dependence, emotional stability and instability, with a high degree of self-awareness. If over-developed, a balanced nature can be upset, sensible introspection can become mental rigidity and fidelity can become obsessive and possessive.

The Mount of the Sun. Apollo's love of beauty and creativity shines like the sun god. A normal or medium mount suggests an artistic soul, as an artist or lover of beauty. Creativity can be expressed in the fine arts, as well as cookery, performing or in the medical field. If over-developed, this mount can suggest a need for pleasure and fame for its own sake. Loving beautiful things can lead to an attraction to surface values. A weak mount suggests a slothful mind, closed to what the world can offer.

The Mounts of Mars. The Upper Mount is best when firm to the touch, which shows self-determination. Courage in personal and work situations is linked to self-esteem and a degree of stubbornness born out of self-preservation. A pronounced mount, raised and very firm to the touch, can take these traits to the limits, with bullying and aggression to the fore. A soft mount suggests that the person is a soft touch and cannot take a firm stance on any issue. The Lower Mount reflects an ability to overcome emotional and physical obstacles. When pronounced, as it is close to the the Mount of Venus, a great sexual appetite can be expected. When under-

developed, there is an underlying timidity and an inabilty to face challenges, either emotional or professional.

The Mount of Luna. This is the guide to the innermost feelings and subconscious drives. It shows our spiritual nature and atavistic feelings. The more pronounced it is, the greater the intuitive and imaginative powers. It also gauges an individual's need and ability to nurture ideas and fellow beings.

FINGERS AND THUMBS

Having formed a general opinion of the hand from its basic form and the relative prominence of the mounts, a study of the fingers provides the first more detailed prognosis of character.

Each finger has particular importance, but must also be considered as an integral part of the hand. Consideration must be given to a comparison with other fingers, length, flexibility, knotting and proportion of the phalanges. For example, if three fingers tend to incline towards the fourth, that will be the dominant influence, therefore if all incline towards Mercury (the little finger) an ability to communicate effectively will be dominant.

A hand with short fingers suggests intuitive gifts, a quick mind able to conquer a new subject, or person, quickly. The whole world will be seen at a glance, often at the expense of essential details.

A hand with long fingers suggests the opposite. Attention to detail comes naturally, without any pedantic qualities. Intellect rules, rather than intuition. Contrary to what their appearance suggests (short would seem more apt) they can be tenacious in a quarrel and are terrier-like in their persistence, especially in relationships.

Smooth fingers, without marked joints, lead to an impulsive nature. Details are of no importance. Obvious facts will be ignored in favour of what the heart or impulsive brain tells them.

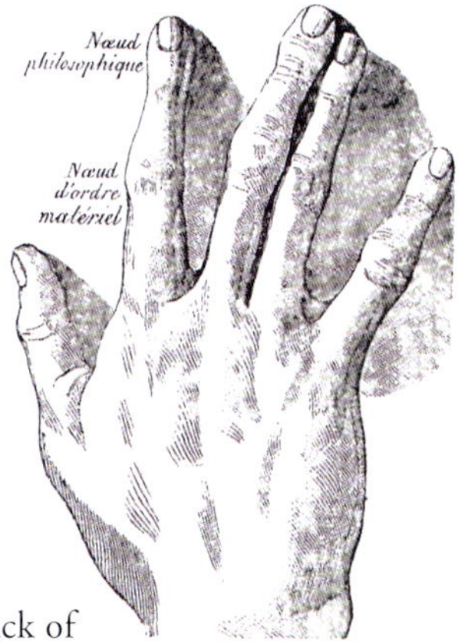

Knotty fingers, when the result of nature and not work or illness, suggest a keen analytical mind. No flights of fancy here. The facts matter and are addressed in a logical way. They may be inventors or innovators, but achieve results through serious research. The lack of a spark of spontaneity can blight personal relationships.

The four fingers are divided into three parts, the phalanges. The top phalange is an indication of mind, the middle phalange is concerned with practicality and the bottom phalange with material matters.

The other general types of finger are:

The Square: A downright, forthright type, loving order and decisive action, though not without foresight and consideration.

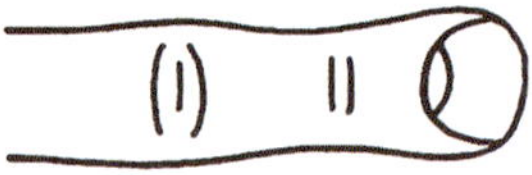

The Spatulate: Suggests energy and self-confidence, though rooted in reality, making for a true confidante in difficult times.

The Conical: A true artistic sign, a taker-in of all ideas and a giver-out of brilliant inspiring thoughts. An ideas person.

The Psychic: Always receptive to others, head in the clouds, but, while there, breathing in psychic and even paranormal thoughts.

The Round: As well-rounded a personality as the shape suggests, balanced in every way, and either deeply emotional or uninvolved – whatever the situation demands.

The Index or **Jupiter** finger shows the need to succeed in life. It should be roughly the same length as Sun and slightly shorter than Saturn. If it is longer than Sun, there may be a touch too much self-esteem, but leadership qualities still abound. If it is shorter than Sun, there is a matching lack of self-confidence. If it veers towards Saturn there may be a tendency to possessiveness of people and property.

The Middle or **Saturn** finger sits between the active digits Jupiter and the thumb, and the more intuitive digits, Sun and Mercury. A straight finger means harmony, whilst veering towards Jupiter suggests extroversion, and towards Sun means introversion, bordering on depression.

The Ring or **Sun** finger indicates artistic tendencies. A long elegant finger is possessed by many who perform, often accentuated by a spatulate tip. If Sun leans too sharply towards Saturn, gullibility is suggested.

The Little or **Mercury** finger rules communication in relationships and business. Ideally it should reach the top phalange of the Sun finger and, when longer, it increases the power to communicate successfully. A short Mercury finger can be an obstacle to getting ideas across or to express oneself emotionally. A slight lean towards Sun suggests diplomacy. A strong lean takes this into the realms of manipulation.

THUMBS UP

The thumb is a powerful indicator of the force of personality and energy levels in general and ego in particular. The length of the thumb is important. The tip should normally reach the lower phalange of the index (Jupiter) finger. A long thumb indicates an overabundance of energy of mind and body. Short thumbs, where the tip falls below the base of the index finger, suggests a complete lack of self-confidence. When reading a thumb, care must be taken to note how it is set on the hand. A low set thumb, at right angles to the palm, shows a mover and shaker. A high set thumb, at a smaller angle originating higher up the palm means that few risks will be taken in business or personal life. The top phalange of the thumb

shows the degree of will power. If spatulate as well (*see Fingers and Thumbs, page 24*), this power is multiplied. The second phalange concerns logic and reasoning.
If emphatic, the ego rules, not always for the best. Self-aggrandisement or self-preservation may prove destructive. If these two phalanges are balanced, thought and action will coincide. Taken with the third phalange, which is the Mount of Venus, the balance of the parts of the thumb can prove a powerful cocktail.

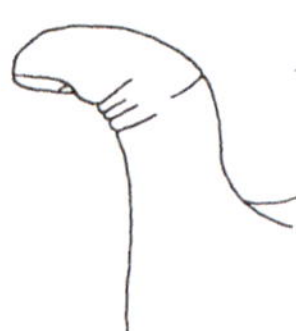

A supple thumb shows an ability to cope, combined with general generosity. A fairly flexible thumb suggests practicality and determination.

A stiff thumb indicates stubbornness and a closed mind. Combined with unfavourable phalanges, this thumb means trouble. Combined with a stunted top phalange and an oblong nail it can mean murder!

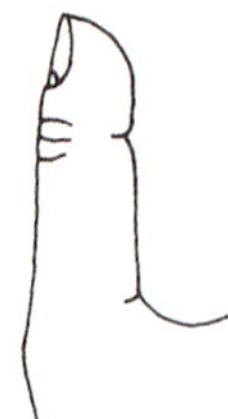

The classic "murderer's" thumb may not spell homicide, but it will suggest an erratic and explosive personality.

The power of the thumb is best expressed by the way it "binds" the hand into a first, the ultimate expression of aggression.

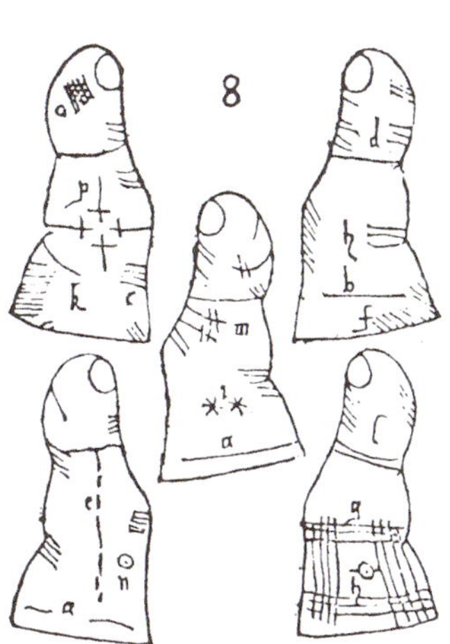

MAIN LINES

The lines are the routes across the hand defining the routes through life. They can indicate time and space, energy and effort, love and lust, war and peace. And, just like life, they can change over weeks and months. Destiny is not carved in stone, but shown in the living flesh of the hand.

What the lines represent physically has never been explained. They appear to serve no particular function, yet are a prominent feature, together with the fingerprints, and are unique to each individual.

Apart from the individual messages to be gleaned

from each line, the number of lines, main and subsidiary, their clarity, the disposition over the hand and colouration have to be taken into account. It would be simplistic to assume that a hand with a few clear main lines would give a particularly clear message. Far from it. It is the relationship of the lines, to each other and the mounts, patternings and breaks which give the deeper message.

The Heart Line, which crosses the top of the palm, can reflect matters of the heart emotionally and physically. A good heart line should be free of islands or breaks (*see Warning Signs, page 39*). Originating below the Mercury finger, it should curve slightly to end between Saturn and Jupiter, which shows a balance of heart and mind. If it splits at the end, this is good as it adds a touch of practicality to the other emotions. A straight heart line suggests a fantasist, a deeply curved one a more physical approach to life and love. If it ends short, under Saturn, more physicality is suggested. If it veers downwards towards the head line, a conflict between intellect and passion is to be expected. If veering away, or far from, the head line, impulsiveness and an unconventional approach to life is heralded.

The Head Line moves almost parallel to the heart line, starting at the life line. It refers to intellect and the psychological base. It can also presage mental problems. A good head line should be clear of imperfections and end with a fork, which denotes balance between fancy and reality. A short line, only reaching the Saturn finger, suggests a concern with pedantic, even boring, matters. A long line suggests a breadth of intellect and emotion. A pale line indicates that all the attributes of the line are weakened. If it has islands, mental problems might have to be faced. A positive sign is when it veers down towards the Mount of Luna, when an almost over-fertile mind can produce fantasies of a wonderful or horrific nature.

The Life Line is regarded as the most important line on the hand. It begins between the thumb and Jupiter finger and arcs downwards, defining the Mount of Venus. As it changes over the years, reading it can be a guide to health, family matters and life expectancy. To predict death

is foolish, as its relationship with other lines matters much. A short life line is of no significance if there are good heart and head lines. In general, a long clear line, sweeping to the wrist, suggests good health and a mental ability to cope with life's problems. When deeply coloured, excessive energy can be added to the previous attributes. If it makes a fulsome arc around the Mount of Venus, life will be sensual until the end. Warm relationships will abound. If it is long, but faint, nagging illnesses will blight life. Islands represent the setbacks through weakness or lack of will. Breaks, which seem ominous, can represent only small setbacks or accidents.

BRANCH LINES

The Girdle of Venus follows the line of the heart at the top of the palm. A rare occurence, its significance lies in highlighting emotional response. Depending on its density it can reflect sexual response from tender caring to rampant promiscuity.

The Inner Life Line, also known as a sister line, runs parallel to the Life Line, offering support and an injection of vitality when needed.

The Simian Line is a fusion of the Heart and Head lines and crosses straight across the palm. This presages a very intense personality which can veer from total dedication to violent conflict of emotions. Which shall rule? Heart or head?

The Line of Saturn is oft-times referred to as the Destiny Line. If clear, well-defined and free of islands or other blemishes, it shows how and when life's aims will be achieved. It is a line much associated with both blue- and white-collar work.

The Line of Apollo is a fairly rare vertical line starting below the Mount of Mercury. It is associated with financial, creative and personal success, which will be

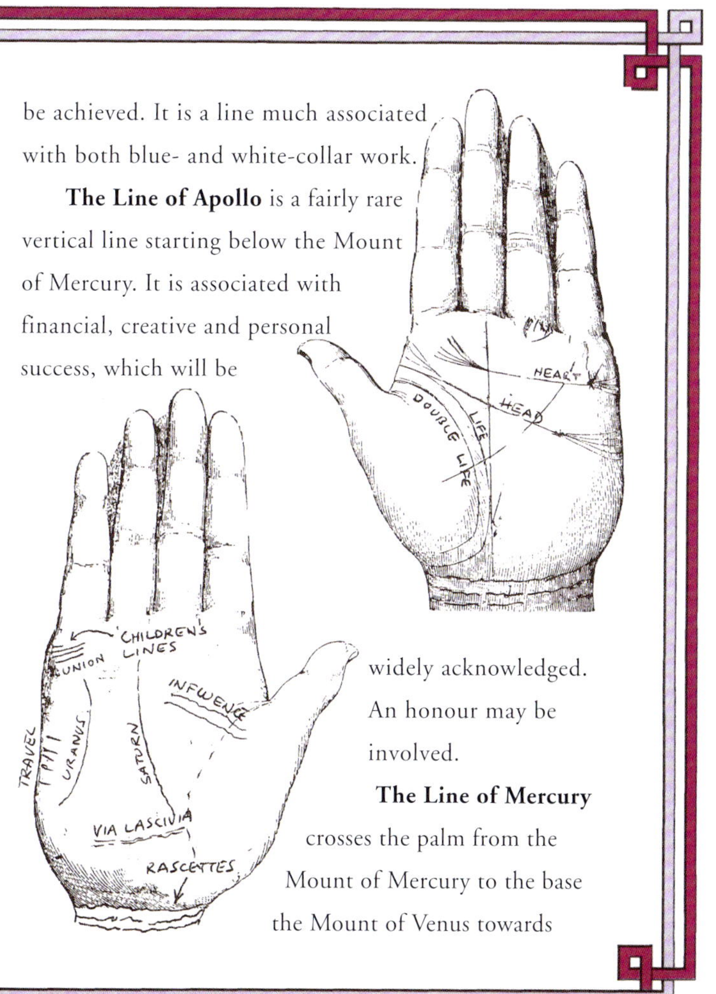

widely acknowledged. An honour may be involved.

The Line of Mercury crosses the palm from the Mount of Mercury to the base the Mount of Venus towards

the ending of the Life Line. It is closely associated with health, particularly digestive problems, which often lie at the root of other problems, which will be elaborated on later (*see page 61*).

The Line of Uranus defines the Mount of Luna, just as the Life Line defines the Mount of Venus, the opposite side of the palm. It almost parallels the Mercury line at places and indicates degrees of intuition which can range from simple awareness to great psychic abilities. It is rarely a complete line as intuition is rarely in continuum.

The Line of Neptune is another rare line, but when it appears it is a powerful indicator of important weaknesses. Also known as the Via Lascivia, it is rarely

other than faint as it breaks away from the Life Line (of which it can appear a part) and moves towards the lower Mount of Mars. It suggests a weakness for alcohol, tobacco and stronger narcotic substances.

The Rascettes of Venus are the lines, usually three, which appear around the wrist, each one representing 30 years of good health. Broken or weak lines have other health implications.

The Lines of Union are small, horizontal, parallel lines, found on the Mount of Mercury. They are sometimes called "marriage lines" as they relate to the important relationships in a lifetime. The deeper the line, the deeper the intensity of the relationship.

The Lines of Influence run parallel to vertical lines such as Life, Saturn and Apollo. They strengthen the influence and act as a link if there is a break in the main line. They can also rise on the Mount of Venus and move across the palm. As they cross other lines they presage trouble. Combined with a dot, island or star, they are warning signs.

WARNING SIGNS

Lines are modified by various markings which appear on them or alongside them. Breaks appear to give an obvious message, but splitting or splintering mark an even greater influence, not always for the bad. They may indicate a new, positive phase. Islands appear as small loops in a line, weakening its strength and dissipating the potential energy generated by the line. Several islands together form a chain leading to a period of serious indecision and wasted emotional and physical resources. When a fork, or split, appears at the end of a line it invariably reveals

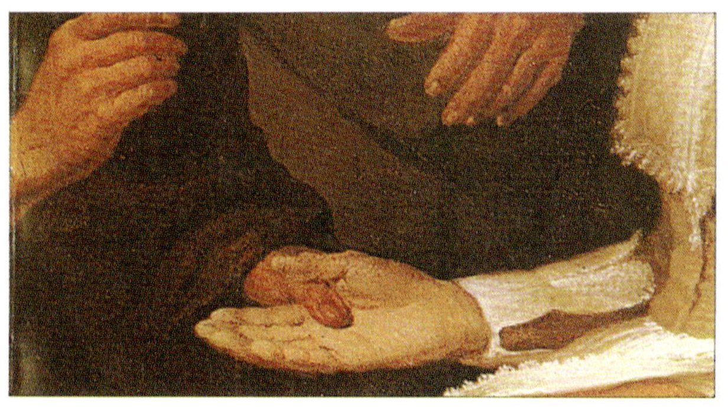

balance, though in conjunction with other signs it can suggest indecision.

A dot is a slight, coloured mark on the line and always suggests a setback, in relationships or health.

A grille, consisting of criss-cross lines, means wasted energy.

A square, often superimposed on a line, intensifies what should be happening at that point in the line. A broken line can be patched together or a vital moment fenced in for protection.

A star, or cluster of stars, heightens the influence of the line or mount on which they appear.

HANDS AT WORK

The hand can provide excellent career guidance, unveiling hidden talents and suggesting new areas to explore. As with astrological predictions, it would be ridiculous to suggest that everyone with a square hand is going to be a son of toil or every conic hand a concert pianist, but with creative thinking a good reading could channel the talents of such hands into unexpected activities.

Square Hands do indeed have a practical bent and are hard workers. They are creative in outdoor pursuits, such as gardening, and indoor pursuits, such as computer programming or office management, where their organisation skills come to the fore. A negative side would be that their love of organisation makes them stick at dull repetitive jobs, when they could achieve so much more.

Spatulate Hands are those of movers and shakers. They get things done, constantly trying to use up a seemingly unstoppable flow of energy. Good organisers, they lean towards leadership and are prepared to take risks. They are often possessed by inventors, either theoretical or practical. This hand is most often masculine and can be associated with sports and sports therapies.

Conical Hands are creative hands pouring out ideas or taking them in with equal alacrity. Unusually for such busy brains, they can work as part of a team, but their input might at times be almost overwhelming. They are

found often in the arts – acting, singing, dancing or designing – and, when tending to an ample consistency, can be creative in fields such as cooking.

Psychic Hands are those of dreamers and visionaries, who can apply their skills in the fields of counselling, psychology or other areas of interpersonal communication. It is also likely that they will veer towards artistic pursuits such as literature, the fine arts or the beauty business.

SPECIAL MARKS

The Medical Hand. When three vertical lines, often crossed by another line, are found on the Mound of Mercury, they indicate a career in the healing professions. Known as the Samaritan lines, even those without medical training can find themselves drawn to the practice of natural medicine or the realms of spiritual healing.

The Travel Hand. When a well-developed Mount of Luna is striated by Samaritan lines, accompanied by a series of small, apparently random lines moving up from its base, the travel

profession is indicated. This can range from being a travel agent, a flight attendant or the pilot of a fighter plane. The small lines also suggest heightened powers of intuition,

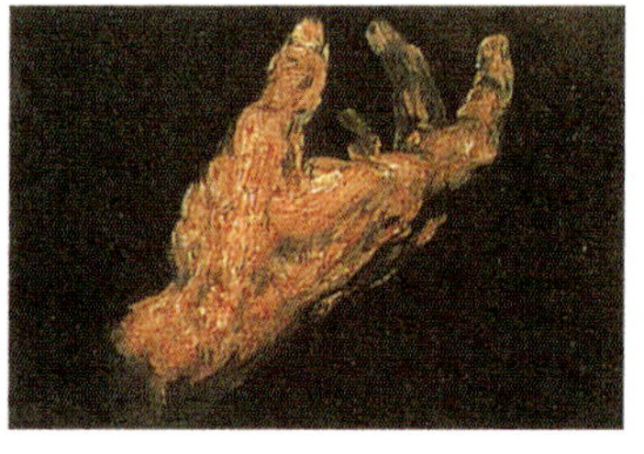

inducing flights of fancy of a psychic kind.

The Land Hand. A square hand has, historically, been associated with farmers or other agriculturalists, often associated with a long base phalange of the Saturn finger. A particular sign would be a pronounced mount of skin entering the palm low down below the Mount of Luna. The love of the country extends to both flora and fauna and there is an intuitive rapport with both.

The Sporting Hand. A well developed and striated Mount of Venus is the mark of those engaged in the sporting field. As it is the seat of energy it is the supporter of a powerful thumb. A matching Mount of Luna doubles the stamina and vitality.

The Pedagogic Hand. Those drawn to the educational profession often have a special series of lines referred to as "the teachers' square". This consists of four small lines forming a cross-hatch square below the Saturn finger. Though not essential for a teacher, it heightens powers of guidance and imparting information. When on the hand of some-one not in the teaching profession, the same powers are often apparent.

Many teachers and lecturers have a Spatulate Hand, intellect being indicated by the length of the first phalange. The longer it is, the more drawn towards theoretical research they are. Indeed, it could even suggest the "perpetual student" syndrome. Similarly, if the joints of the fingers are pronounced, they will be drawn to work of a philosophical nature.

HAND IN HAND

As analysis of the hand helps achieve a deeper degree of self-awareness, it should, in turn, help create meaningful and lasting relationships. And, during those relationships, warn of rocky passages and other possible pitfalls.

Certain forms of hands are compatible with each other, whilst others suggest a stormy passage. The combinations are immense, but some basic relationships can give a general guide. A Square Hand with a Square Hand suggests a relationship based on mutual practicality. Square with Conic is promising, as Square can bring Conic down to earth, but Conic's impulsiveness can lead to upheavals. Square with Spatulate definitely get on, making for a highly creative couple. Square with Psychic promises a sticky, if not volcanic, end.

Conic with Conic could prove mutually exciting, as could be a pairing with Spatulate. With a Psychic hand creative juices will be stimulated, Conic bringing a little reality into Psychic's life.

Spatulate with Spatulate encourages mutual imagination, with a practical touch, like a pair of ballroom dancers. Spatulate with Psychic is best avoided altogether.

Psychic with Psychic will end up living in the clouds, which may be no bad thing, but don't expect them to arrive on time, if they turn up at all.

ALL FINGERS AND THUMBS

The digits add the next layer of understanding in relationships. The angle of the thumb is a clear indication of sexual inhibition. A high set thumb shows some inhibitions and, as the angle increases, these are released. When the angle in relation to the Jupiter finger exceeds ninety degrees complete openness in sexual matters is assured, making for easy relationships. A strong thumb may well succeed with a weak thumb, who may well wish to be dominated. Strong thumb with strong thumb may get on through mutual admiration, but battles may well be expected. Two weak thumbs will just drift along together.

Long fingers with long fingers suggest a plodding relationship, but sincere. Short fingers with short fingers create a sparkling relationship, a little self-absorbed, but great fun. Long fingers with short fingers, which look after the grand plan, is a good match, provided that the long fingers are allowed to look after the details. Knuckled fingers with smooth fingers makes for an abrasive relationship.

Loners, who do not actively seek relationships, often have square fingertips. Widely spread fingers, which show an extrovert personality, could have a riotous time with a similar partner, but related to tightly closed fingers might have a tendency to dominate. The reserved closed fingers could find a relationship with a similar hand a source of endless unspoken grudges and secret regrets.

ALONG THE SAME LINES

It is often sufficient to read only one person's hand to determine how they will perform in a relationship, though comparing hands can often help avoid some obvious clashes. The Heart Line is the best indicator. Ideally, it should cut clear across the top of the hand, without any blemishes. If it ends by curving generously towards the Jupiter finger, stopping between it and Saturn, a balanced personality is suggested, one who will blend harmoniously with most others. They will try their best to make things work. If it veers more towards Jupiter itself, there will be a certain vulnerability, combined with unrealistic expectations. Their love can turn to obsession. A line directed towards the thumb suggests a self-obsessed person who will find it hard to establish relationships as work and self will come first. A straight, clear line ending under the Saturn finger indicates sexual desire taking

precedence over deeper love. These simplified explanations are refined, usually not for the best, by islands, chains, dots or other blemishes.

The Head Line indicates the practicalities of relationships and as such can be a better guide to business life. Once the line is examined it gives an idea of the practical approach to the world, which would then need to be compared to that of a prospective partner. For example, an extremely curved Head Line, indicating great mood swings, might not get on with a straight line, which denotes a pragmatic approach to life.

Lines which cross the Destiny Line presage the timing of the end of a relationship. Lines which touch and merge with it time the consolidation of a relationship, though if this line has islands, it may be a fraught and brief liaison.

The clarity of the Destiny Line when it meets a branch, usually arising on the Mount of Luna, shows the effect a relationship has on the subject. If it remains clear, then the relationship will strengthen, if it becomes stronger there can be improvement in general, and consolidation if there was trouble on the horizon. If it weakens, or becomes afflicted by islands or breaks, problems are impending. A branch line arising on the Mount of Luna and running parallel to the Destiny Line suggests a particularly fruitful relationship.

Similar lines can parallel the Life Line with the Mount of Venus. This strengthens any relationship, but its length does not relate to the length of that relationship.

Marriage, which was regarded as the ultimate relationship, has been thought to be indicated by horizontal lines just under the Mercury finger, but in an age of many different types of relationships, their meaning is now more ambiguous. They can indicate the ending of a good relationship by tragic death if they break into the Heart Line. Small lines between them were thought to represent children, but can also indicate an empathy with young people, such as you might find in a teacher or indulgent relative.

For some years it was thought that same-sex orientation could be detected in the hand, but this involved many out-dated assumptions; soft hands, pointed fingers and supple thumbs suggesting homosexuality. A chained Heart Line and a broken girdle of Venus, representing unstable emotions and overt sexuality, theoretically confirmed such suspicions. In an age of greater freedom of sexual orientation, when assessing hands for partnership, no dogmatic approach should be pursued.

HANDS ACROSS THE AGES

Compatibility can be assessed by comparing the lines on the hand. The most famous recorded example is that of Napoleon and his Empress, Josephine. Long before they met, when Josephine was bathing in a stream in her native Martinique, an old negress was attracted by the shape of her hands. She read Josephine's palm and predicted that she would become "more famous than a queen". Napoleon's hand shows the strong thumb of a masterful person, with auspicious triple stars on it and, at the join with the palm, the even fingers of determination and persistence, together with a firm Life Line. He was, after all, not to die in battle, but of poison.

Josephine's hand has a delicate thumb at a more pronounced angle away from the first finger, which suggests compatability with, and not domination by, Napoleon. The curious angling of the middle fingers suggests fidelity; fate beckons in the broken Life Line with its star burst and a large Mount of Luna.

Their shared charisma, inspiration and ambition is embodied in equally emphatic Mounts of Jupiter.

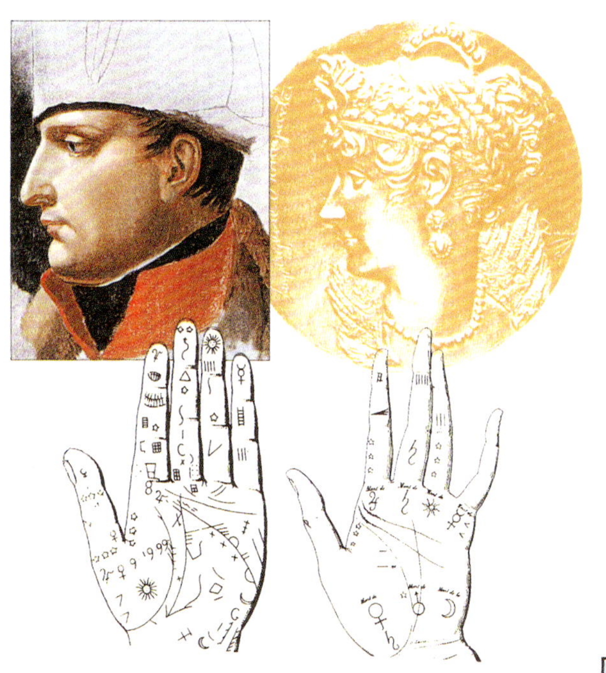

HEALTH IN THE HAND

Firm predictions based on the lines and mounds of the hand are not advised. Health is the most important matter for most people, and to add to any worries by predicting a specific disease, the precise length of life or impending mental problems is ill-advised. The hand should be regarded as a guide to tendencies affecting health, a warning to slow down or to take necessary precautions. A long Life Line does not necessarily mean that you will not be knocked down by a car. The hand cannot predict the unpredictable.

As we have previously noted, the pattern of lines on the hand, the texture of the mounts and the overall colouration, a key indicator, can change over relatively short periods.

Colour: A roseate hue is normal on hands of all races, which indicates good blood circulation and normal bodily functions. A deep red hue suggests a tendency to high blood pressure, other blood related problems such as gout and the possibility of diabetes in later life.

A pale hand, especially when allied to cold and clammy palms, suggests anxiety-related illness and warns to take precautions regarding insipient anaemia.

Warm hands with a veiny blue appearance can also suggest anaemia and bad reactions to certain medications. Cold, bluish hands counsel a visit to your doctor.

Hands with a jaundiced appearance show weakness of the liver, with the attendant diseases such as hepatitis.

The lines, their imperfections, the mounts and the nails give invaluable advice and warnings about many present or impending ailments.

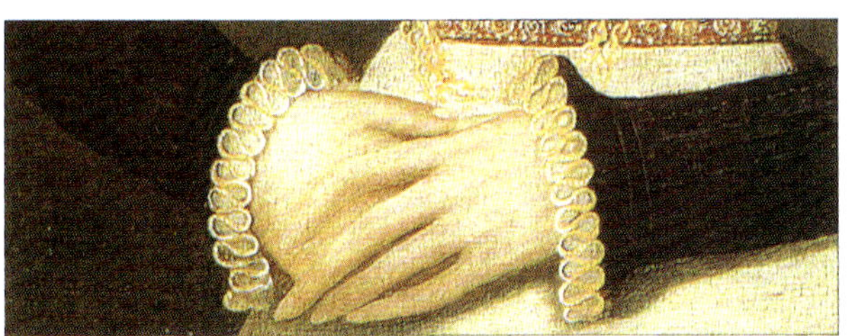

Allergies: The hand cannot identify specific allergies as there is a plethora of causes, many of a short-term nature. Areas of the hand which can help are strongly ridged nails, when related to the Line of Neptune. Appearing together they warn of adverse reaction to drugs and, indeed, dependence or misuse of them.

Cardiovascular problems: The colour of the nails can suggest irregularities, especially when they have a bluish tinge. Naturally, brightly coloured nails are no better, as they suggest an overbearing temperament, which could lead to heart problems. Reading the islands, dots or other imperfections on the Heart Line, can warn of heart problems. A chain of islands is very debilitating and, when accompanied by dots, accentuates the seriousness and increases the possibilty of those problems. Take medical advice.

Deficiences: The nails are good indicators. White specks mark a calcium deficiency, also indicated by brittleness. When the Heart and Head Lines are heavily islanded it would be wise to investigate possible mineral deficiencies. A pale palm and lines suggest an iron deficiency and often appears after menstruation.

Digestion: An excess of small lines, like a monster grille, interfering with the Mercury line in particular, presages digestive problems, often arising out of an unsuitable or deficient diet. Broken, pitted or deformed nails are a well-known sign of bad eating habits.

Eyes, Teeth and Ears: The Heart Line is the major indicator of problems in these areas. An island under the Apollo finger suggests impending sight problems, and when accompanied by a grille above, it presages dental problems. With a further island between the mounts of Jupiter and Saturn, ear problems may need attention. It has been suggested that these marks should be checked on children's hands as minor hearing and sight problems can often go undetected.

Headaches: The Head Line can mark problems such as migraine, which often occurs when there are indentations. A broad line, or one with a strong sister line, suggests dizziness leading to muddled thinking and lack of concentration. Anxiety, leading to head problems, is emphasized by islands in the Life Line.

Reproduction: Internal weaknesses of the reproductive system are often indicated by a wildly erratic top rascette, which can loop up almost onto the palm. Male uro-genital problems and female gynaecological complications are marked by a cross-hatching, like a large grille, on the outside of the Life Line. A check-up is advised.

Respiratory system: The whole range of chest problems from chills to pneumonia is indicated by islands on the Life Line. As children have fewer imperfections on these lines, if they appear illness may well dog the early years. Combined with islands on the Mercury line the position is exacerbated. Small moons on the nails suggest lung problems, a feature reported as occurring often on the hands of heavy smokers.

Stress: The number of lines, no matter their appearance, indicate the sensitivity of the person concerned, leading to stress and anxiety. Taking on unnecessary responsibilities leads to further stress. Lines across the top of the fingers indicate added anxiety. Those on the Jupiter finger concern worries about personal standing; on the Saturn finger they presage worries about a career; on the Apollo finger they dim the natural sunniness; and on the Mercury finger they cloud self-expression and cause problems in sexual relationships. These lines usually appear in varying degrees; the finger with the heaviest degree of marking will point the way. For example, if the Saturn finger is heavily marked and the Apollo finger even more so, there is the suggestion of serious family or relationship problems. These lines can come and go quite quickly. Those on the objective hand change quicker than those on the subjective hand, thus enabling the timing of the particular problem to be ascertained. The flexibilty of the palm can also be a marker of stress. If it curves easily outwards under the Mercury finger, it can indicate an overactive mind, people who live on their nerves' edge. Calm down.

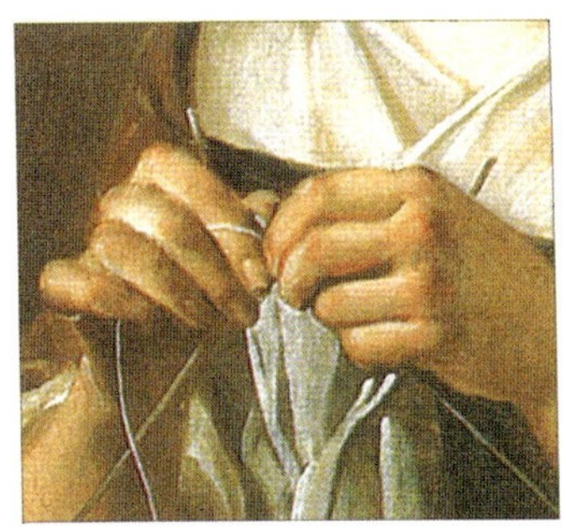

ACKNOWLEDGEMENTS

Illustrations are from the Libraire Viollet, Paris, Hulton Picture Library, Bibliotheque National (Giraudet) Paris, Folksmuseum, Holstebro, Denmark, the Corcoran Collection, London, and Grapharchive, London.
Hand maps re-created by Cosway Graphics.
The publishers have made every effort to identify all illustration sources. Any errors and omissions will be corrected in future editions.